DALKEY
County Dublin

GUIDE
TO THE HISTORIC
TOWN OF
DALKEY

containing information on

First published 1996
This edition in 2001

MORRIGAN BOOKS
KILLALA, CO.MAYO

© Conan Kennedy

ISBN 0 907677 58 4

The modern placename Dalkey derives from the Irish word Dealg, *meaning thorn, and the Scandanavian word for Island,* Ey, *thus called from the early custom of building thorny barricades around settlements. While the Norse were said to have had a fort on the island, it was a stronghold far earlier (see below).*

Originally the name Dalkey referred only to the actual island, the adjacent mainland being known as Kilbegnet, *Begnet's Church. The modern Irish language name for Dalkey is* Deilginis, *inis being the Irish for Island.*

DALKEY - EARLIEST ORIGINS ...

While no structures survive from earliest times within the Dalkey area, there is no doubt that, with its distinctive hills facing the rising sun across the sea, this anchoring place must have been an important site from remotest antiquity. Archaeological investigation has shown that Dalkey Island was already inhabited around 4000BC. A dolmen still exists in the adjoining area of Ballybrack and records do remain on Dalkey's own lost antiquities.

The ancient church on Dalkey Island is said to have been built from the stones of the *Dún* or Fort of Sedgha, a Milesian ruler. These Milesians, of Spanish origin, came to Ireland perhaps around 500BC. Mythological sources have it that they earlier originated in Egypt.

Even earlier settlement is confirmed by the fact that, up until around 1800AD there was a dolmen within a stone circle on Dalkey Common. These stones were blown up in the nineteenth century and used to construct the Martello Tower at Bartra. Also, until the 1840's, there was a large boulder *(illus.page 29)* on the top of Dalkey Hill known as Clogh-tobber-geleen, a phrase derived from Irish which could be translated as "The Stone of The Well of the Gallion." These *gallion* were a powerful Leinster tribe of mercenaries associated in proto-history with Queen Medb. Another link with the remotest past is the fact that, on nearby Killiney Hill it is still a folk custom to walk clockwise round one of the structures, for luck. This is a rite, common in modern Ireland, which derives from ancient sunworshippers.

An early engraving of Dalkey. The Castle on the right is now part of the Town Hall, that in background on left is Archbold's Castle *(also illus.on front cover)*. The town stocks are shown on left, at the entrance to the presentday church car park. The thatched cottage on extreme right is close by the Queens Pub and may have been part of the 1715 inn known as 'The House of The Red Cross'.
Remnants of this inn are now the rere part of the Queens Off Licence and adjoining interiors shop.

Dalkey Island and the adjacent coastline were part of the territory of Cualu. The first mention of the place refers to events in the early eighth century AD and then in the tenth century when Coibhdeanach, Abbot Cill-achaidh, fled to Dalkey Island from the Norsemen in 939AD. Five years later the Irish burnt the Norse settlement of Dublin and it was the turn of the Norse themselves to flee here by boat.

After the Norman invasion Dalkey was 'granted' in 1176 to the Archbishop by a Norman leader Hugo de Lacy. However it had also been given, five years earlier, to the Priory of Holy Trinity (later Dublin's Christ Church Cathedral) by Donagh or Fat Donald. His correct name was Mac-GillaMocholmoc, and he was the Irish chieftain of Cuala.

The subsequent confusion over ownership led first to the excommunication of all associated with the Priory and then to a Papal Court's decision that, while the Priory owned the Church itself, the Archdeacon had a 'Right of Visitation'. He also maintained the essential point of the argument, namely the lordship and manorial rights to the area. Ownership remained in the hands of the Church until it dissipated over the sixteenth and seventeenth centuries.

DALKEY - THE MODERN TOWN...

Dalkey is located some eight miles south east of Dublin City on the coast. Administratively it is now part of Dublin County and, indeed, outlying areas of Dalkey merge into the adjoining suburbs. However, situated off the main routes and protected on one side by the sea and its beaches, and by wooded hills on the other, Dalkey retains a distinctive separate character. The heart of Dalkey for hundreds of years has been Castle Street and a visit to the town should be started here.

Both the DART and Dublin Bus leave the visitor within yards of the centre. And for people arriving by car, whilst parking in the centre is difficult, there are large free public car parks both beside the Catholic Church and to the rear of the supermarket, accessed from beside Allied Irish Banks.

Modern Castle Street

This, with its extension Railway Road, is the commercial hub of the town. The buildings as seen to-day largely date from the second half of the nineteenth century, though parts of these would be reconstructions of much earlier houses and cottages. With the presence of large centres such as DunLaoghaire nearby the use of Dalkey's buildings has changed to the mix seen to-day. On the upper floors, where families of shopkeepers and tradespeople once lived, there are now numerous small business though, among them, there are still a few flats and apartments. The great bulk of residents of the town itself live in the small streets and roads to the north of Castle Street, while many more people live in the wider general areas known as Dalkey. This is a mixed area ranging in style from roads of magnificent Victorian mansions to estates of modern housing.

Church in Castle Street,
as drawn by J.P.O'Reilly in 1900.

DALKEY - THE ANCIENT CHURCHES

While the most obvious structures to the visitor are the castles (see page 12), the churches belong to a far earlier era. The origins of Dalkey are essentially religious and, as noted earlier, are rooted in Stone Circles and the like and, in more approachable times, with the beginning of Christianity in these parts.

Dalkey has the remains of two Early Christian churches, both dedicated to St Begnet, a woman saint (see page 10) One of these churches is on the island, the other is in Castle Street in the centre of the town.

St Begnet's Church,

(Castle Street)

This church was built at two periods, the nave or western end being the original, the eastern chancel being added at a later period. Certain architectural features imply that the earliest portion may have replaced a wooden church. The bell tower *(illustrated on facing page)* is of a type where access was gained by steps, the bells being struck rather than pulled by ropes. It has been suggested that this feature, common in early Spanish churches, may indicate a connection between the early religious here and Spain *(see below)*. The two parts of the church are not in a straight line, this slight kink being a mediaeval device to imply the bowing of Christ's head on the Cross. The general alignment of early churches was such as to allow them to face the rising sun on the feast day of their patron saint. Any alignment will give this effect on two days of the year, and in the case of this church one of those days is appropriate to St Begnet and the other to another holy person, Lughaid, described as her brother.

St Begnet's Church,

(Dalkey Island)

This church is of the very earliest Christian *Cill* or cell type. The same word gives the prefix to those many Irish placenames starting with Kill-. Neighbouring Killiney takes its name from the Irish for 'Church of the daughters of Leinin'. It would thus appear that many early Christian leaders along this coastline were women.

In the nineteenth century the workers on the military structures on the island used this church as a house, and it was they who built the fireplace and chimney. The church is surrounded by a graveyard of which no surface trace remains.

The orientation of the church is different to that in the town, and this suggests that it may have been originally dedicated to a different saint or, indeed, built for a different purpose. Calculations have been made which appear to show that the position of the original window would have been useful for calculating the calendar by solar observation. The church was built by masons using the Spanish unit of measurement, the *Vara* or Castilian Yard.

Church on Dalkey Island,
as drawn by W.Wakeman in 1891.

St Begnet's Graveyard. . .

The earliest readable headstone in this now disused graveyard is dated 1738, but there are burials from far earlier periods, many unmarked. It is estimated that upwards of 2000 people may be buried here.

The Rathdown Slab *(see page 26)* was discovered here in 1835. Also (but now buried and lost again!) there was a small pagan pillarstone *(illustrated on right)* with finger holes, similar to those found at other very early church sites.

St Begnet

The folklore of north-western England frequently mentions a saint by the name of Bega. She is said to have lived in the mid-seventh century and, after the intervening twelve hundred years, it is understandable that records are slight, and those that do exist are sometimes contradictory, and that many of her attributes and doings have been borrowed from other saints of other periods. In the Irish context Bega was associated with a priest known as Lughaidh, and both were described as 'Children of Gauran'. Early Christian leaders were married and Lughaid could very well have been her husband. (The description of early women religious leaders as 'virgin' was appropriate to later dogmas). A place in Meath, associated with St Patrick, was described as 'Bega's Tomb'. Many places in north west England and Scotland can trace their names to Bega, but she was particularly associated with islands and remote spots.

Folklore explains by simplifying complex themes into understandable stories. Bega, it is said, was an Irish princess who fled an unwanted suitor and embraced Christianity in Britain. On one of her missionary trips about the place she founded a religious settlement in Dalkey. She died in England.

Dalkey's Modern Churches:

St Begnet's Church on the island had certainly been abandoned before the 12th century, and that in Dalkey Town fell into disuse in the 17th century. Although in the early 19th century there was a chapel house in Sorrento Road, and earlier there had been a similar meeting place in Barnhill Road, there was no proper church at all in the immediate locality until the construction of the two new 19th century buildings.

Church of the Assumption,
Roman Catholic:

In **Castle Street**, originally this was a simple structure consisting of the present nave, completed in 1841. Around fifty years later the transepts and tower were added. These are built in cut stone, in contrast to the rendered rubble of the original portion, this signifying the growing wealth and numbers of the Catholic population. The whole church was renovated in 1991.

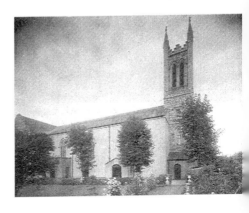

St Patrick's Church,
Church of Ireland:

In **Church Road,** which connects Ulverton to Harbour Road, this church opened in 1843. The building is the result of an architectural competition won by a Mr Jacob Owen, and it cost £1600 to build, a not inconsiderable sum at the time. The stone was quarried right beside the site, and that quarry is now the site of the fine 'Russian Villa' style rectory, built in 1866.

St Patrick's Church

Dalkey Buildings

Apart from the churches there are no major public buildings in Dalkey, though there is no shortage of attractive interesting architecture. The facade of the old **Library** (1901) is preserved as part of the front of the supermarket. Notable also is the former bank, now **Vico Interiors** in Castle Street, and **Dalkey Pharmacy** in Railway Road. The **News Centre** was the (1894) **Leinster Tea Rooms,** and the **Select Stores** was **The Railway Hotel.** The **Health Centre** was built as **Dalkey Dispensary** (1909). In Patricks Road the **Urban Cottages** are interesting, as is the **Harold Boys School,** typical of that period. **Kent Terrace** is vaguely tudor in style, much like the family that built it in 1839.

DALKEY - THE CASTLES

The castles are more correctly described as fortified warehouses, and they date from the 15th-16th centuries. Originally there is said to have been seven, and evidence exists for most of these, though it should be remembered that in folklore the notion of towns having seven castles was common in earlier periods. One of the now vanished castles, Dongan's Castle, stood at the bus shelter opposite Kent Terrace. Thomas Dongan, of this family, was Governor of New York in 1682-91. The stones of this castle were used to build Kent Terrace.

Three castles survive in Dalkey, two in the town and the third at Bullock.

Goat Castle in now the Town Hall. It takes its name from the fact that its original owners, a family called Cheevers, had a goat featured in their family crest. Of Norman origin, the family name could be based on the french word *Chevre*, meaning goat.

Archbold's Castle on the opposite side of the street(*illustrated on front cover*) takes its name from onetime owners of adjoining lands.

Bullock Castle (*illus.right*) on Ulverton Road outside the town was constructed by Cistercian Monks to protect their fishery interests. It is now part of a Retirement Home.

As drawn by Wakeman, 1896

DALKEY - MILITARY STRUCTURES

In addition to the castles, which were defensive rather than military, there are a number of surviving military structures from various periods. Archaeologists note evidence of a pre-historic Promontary Fort on Dalkey Island but the average person will see no trace of such. The main feature on Dalkey Island is a much later structure, one of Dalkey's two

Martello Towers

These towers, which take their name from a structure in Corsica, were built by the British as a coastal defence against an expected Napoleonic invasion. There are many examples of them on both the north and south of Dublin City and they are also to be found on the Shannon River and on coastlines in Britain itself. The Dalkey towers are almost identical to that at Adaya in Minorca, and all are believed to be designed by the British engineer Captain Birch.

Dalkey Island Tower, 'Number Nine' to its military builders, is a typical and well-preserved example. It was built around 1804 at a then cost of £2000, perhaps £200,000 in our money! The military, then as now, did not believe in penny pinching. Essentially the towers were a combination of look-out point and gun emplacement. Each tower along the coast was in visual contact with the next and thus messages could be passed back and forth. The top of this tower held two 24-pounder cannons on a swivel beam, and the tracking for this can still be observed. These guns had a range of a mile, and the shot could be heated red hot to set rigging of ships on fire. Internally the tower was divided into quarters for a garrison and stores for munitions.

It is said of the Dalkey Island tower that, long after the threat of invasion had passed, the garrison were forgotten by the military authorities and continued to draw food and pay for years of idleness, during which they married local girls, raised families and kept goats.

Bullock Tower,
'Number Ten', is on private lands at Bartra near Bullock Harbour, and nearby at Sandycove the so called **'Joyces Tower'** is another example.

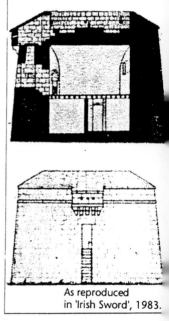

Section and Elevation of Bullock Tower,
note thickness of walls compared to internal space.

As reproduced in 'Irish Sword', 1983.

Artillery Batteries:

The structure at the southern tip of the island is a battery for artillery, constructed at the same period as the tower. While it doesn't look much from the shore, or indeed, from outside, internally can be seen evidence of fine military stonework and engineering, including the semicircular swivel tracks of the guns.

In Sorrento Park are the remains of another battery, this one built during the period known in Ireland as 'the emergency', in the rest of the world as the Second World War. At the highest point of the ground in the park can be seen a circular brick plinth, the base of an anti-aircraft gun emplacement. The nearby low concrete walls are the remains of the soldiers' hut.

On Dalkey Hill the castle-like structure is in fact the remains of an 1807 Semaphore Tower. From here great windmill like vanes were used to pass signals back and forth between ships in the bay and military HQ in Dublin City.

Walls of Dalkey:

Dalkey and Bullock were separate walled towns. There is no trace of these walls as such but suggestions are made that, in fact, several of the vanished 'seven castles' were in fact gate towers. The main entrance to the town would have been beside the present-day post office, and the eastern wall was across the far end of the street near the bank. On the south side of the town the defences were in the form of earthworks and traces of these can be seen at the entrance to Hillside Estate on Dalkey Avenue. A location on Vico Road, near the Railway Bridge, is still known locally as 'The Ramparts'.

From a period far earlier than these structures, there is some vague evidence that Dalkey Hill itself may have been a fortified site. Mercenary groupings such as the Gallion, whose well was on the hill, *(see pages 28 & 29)* based themselves in such locations. In the woods at the top of the Burma Road can be seen traces of ancient ditches around the hill's perimeter. Early maps noted a now vanished 'mound', perhaps burial, at this spot.

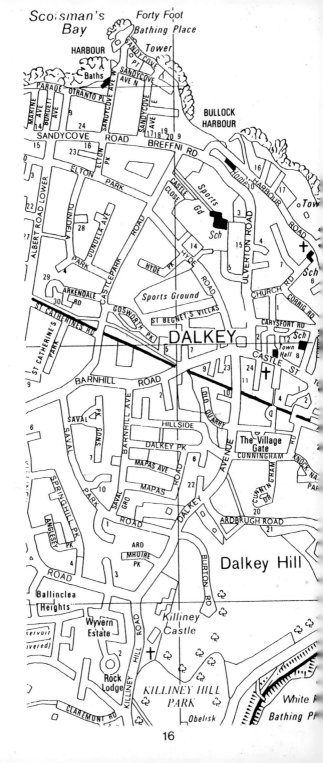

DALKEY

&

SURROUNDING AREAS

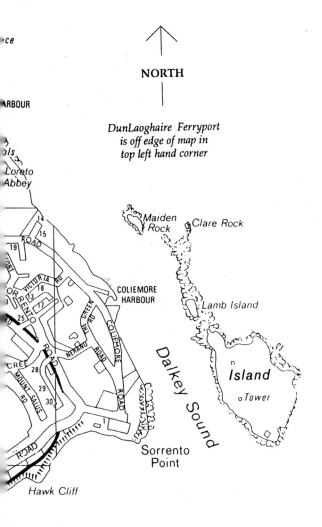

↑

NORTH

*DunLaoghaire Ferryport
is off edge of map in
top left hand corner*

ce

RBOUR

ls

*Loreto
Abbey*

Maiden
Rock

Clare Rock

14

15

19

VICTORIA RD

18

ORRENTO

13

25

THE GREEN RD

NERANO ROAD

COLIEMORE HARBOUR

Lamb Island

Island

Tower

CREE

28

ROAD

COLIEMORE ROAD

29

MOUNT SALUS RD

30

Dalkey Sound

ROAD

Sorrento
Point

Hawk Cliff

DALKEY ISLAND

Dalkey Island is an area of some 25 acres and has some small adjacent islets. These, to the north, are Lamb Island, Clare Island, and Maiden Rock. The latter's name is said to originate from the drowning of some girls there while gathering edible seaweeds. *(The illustration on right shows a 19th century view)*

Archaeological investigation has shown that the island was occupied from a very early period, intermittent settlements being noted from the neolithic to the bronze ages. Burials from these periods have been unearthed, including a human skull that was filled with seashells for some ritual purpose.

In the early Christian era it was, remains indicate, in touch with many parts of Europe. Finds include 5th and 6th century glass from France or Belgium, English pottery of the 13th century, and an 11th century Normandy silver coin. The banks and ditches still faintly outlined are the remains of field systems of varying ages, some fields being used for tillage, others for grazing. The North West corner, (that is the part to the left of the landing looking from the shore,) was a Promontary Fort, defended by a ditch and bank. Technical evidence from charcoal discovered on the island shows that it was in the early Christian era made up largely of wood from the holly tree . . .this may be another reason for the name Thorn Island.

To the north-east is **The Muglins,** an island with a small automatic shipping beacon.

In the early eighteenth century two pirates, McKinley and Zekerman, were hung in chains here. They had hijacked a ship in the Canary Islands, murdered the captain and raped his wife, and were caught in Dublin. Crime was taken more seriously then than now and they were hung in chains in the city. However the rotting flesh disturbed the noses of the gentry and so the corpses were moved to The Muglins.

Killiney Hill & Bay, from a lithograph of 1869.

SEASIDE & BEACHES

For a town on the sea, it is surprisingly difficult to get close to water in Dalkey. Much of the coast is built up and is private grounds and, apart from the harbours (overleaf) there are few spots for the visitor to actually put toes into the water. The nearest to the town is **Dillon's Park,** which is a lot larger than it appears from the road. This is not a swimming place but people can scramble along by water's edge or fish from the rocks with rod and line. **Vico Bathing Place** was formerly for 'Gentlemen Only' and still retains some aspects of that distinction. The bathing place is accessible down a signposted cliff walk off Vico Road.

Further up Vico Road another walk leads down to **White Rock Beach,** a beautiful sandy little place with safe bathing. Popular with families, there are rock pools and places for children to explore in reasonable safety. Don't let them go too far into the cave or too far up the cliffs. Deco's Cave is part of a mineshaft, taking its name from a 19th century eccentric resident of the cave, Deco Kavanagh.

This beach is actually an extension of **Killiney Beach** and the energetic can walk for literally miles along to the south without having to worry about walking back, there are DART stations almost on the beach at Killiney and Shankill.

DALKEY - THE HARBOURS

Dalkey developed as a port because it was at the time Dublin's nearest safe deep water anchorage. The city's harbour itself at the time was unsuitable due to silting and sandbars. Another and perhaps equally important factor was because, by using Dalkey with its different authorities, merchants could circumvent various taxes and regulations.

Ships from British ports such as Chester, Falmouth and Bristol, and from the continental European ports, mainly French but also Spanish and Dutch, anchored in the sound and goods were transported either to land at Dalkey or to smaller boats to take them on to Dublin. A significant trade used Dalkey as a transhipment point from Europe to Britain. Dalkey's period as the main port of Dublin spanned the 14th to 17th centuries.

Coliemore Harbour was the landing point and the modern-day Coliemore Road follows the route across the then Dalkey Commons to the town. Goods going to Dublin from here went along the ancient route now marked by the modern Barnhill Road.

Bullock Harbour developed around the separate fishery town, with its own walls and administration, of Bullock. The name is variously described as having evolved from Irish language words, meaning either 'sandbanks' or 'the characteristic booming sound of waves'. Perhaps more relevant is the fact that there was, on the south-east tip of Dalkey Island, a great 'rocking stone' in a depression beneath the tide line. This gave out a great booming sound with the action of waves and was known as 'The Devil's Mill'.

Coliemore Harbour (illustrated above with the island in the background) to-day is the main point of embarkation for the Island. Boats can be hired here and there is also a ferry service back and forth.

Bullock Harbour is a centre for fishing and the hire of fishing boats.

DALKEY - THE RAILWAY

Ireland's first real railway linked Dublin and DunLaoghaire and was opened in 1834. At around the same time DunLaoghaire harbour was being constructed and there was already a type of rail line linking the harbour site to the Dalkey quarries. This was operated by gravity, the laden trucks of rock coming down being used to simultaneously haul the empties back up again. (At the quarries in Ardbrugh Road the grooves cut by cables in the rock can still be

seen). In 1841, with the harbour almost completed, the major part of the route between Dalkey and DunLaoghaire was sold to a company who built the 'Atmospheric Railway' along part of the  route. (Original cuttings associated with this route can be seen at Castle Park Road). This railway was operated by a vacuum tube and, instead of having engines, the trains were 'sucked' along, the vacuum being created by a fixed engine at the end of the line. This opened in 1844 to general amazement and technological enthusiasm. It ran successfully for ten years before being replaced by the extension of the conventional railway, first from DunLaoghaire to Dalkey, and then onwards down the east coast. Extensive new cuttings were built but alongside these there remains a pedestrian pathway known locally as The Metals, this taking its name from and being the remnants of the original stone carrying line. It is possible to walk this route from DunLaoghaire Station to the top of Dalkey Hill. The latter part of the route is known as 'The Flags', from the distinctive original granite paving flags along the way.

Construction of the railway tunnel at Dalkey, photographed in 1877. The modern DART passes through here en route to Killiney Bay.

The Dalkey Tram

The last electric tram ran to Dalkey from Dublin in 1949. The route was identical to that of the present number eight bus. The tramway was at first horse-drawn, later electrified. At Bullock Castle in horse-drawn days an additional horse waited to be hitched on to help the vehicles climb the hill.

Little signs of the tramway remain but here and there along the route there are distinctive iron lamp standards which originally held the overhead wires. In Dalkey Town there is the well preserved tram stables and depot, now a woodworking factory. Inside the gates the tracks and distinctive granite tram 'sets' can still be seen. Behind the Town Hall there are some streets of brick cottages which were originally built by the tram company for their workers. Many of the present occupants of these are descendants of tram drivers and conductors.

DALKEY - VICTORIAN TIMES

Dalkey as seen to-day is, essentially, a nineteenth century town. In that century, from being an almost abandoned and quite derelict former port, it grew dramatically under two major influences. Firstly there was the influx of quarry workers associated with the huge construction works of DunLaoghaire harbour. And, secondly, with a more lasting impact on the nature of to-day's town, there was the construction of numerous grand residences in the area as, opened up by the railway, Dalkey became a desirable place to live for the Dublin merchant classes. Many of these houses started life as smaller summer residences, others were built from scratch by entrepreneurs. Practically all were built on former common lands. People in outlying cabins and cottages were bought out and, for a period right up to the nineteen twenties, Dalkey town itself was grossly overcrowded and suffered poor living conditions for ordinary people. All this was far from the world of the big houses.

Because of the hilly nature of the area, and because most were built to take advantage of the views, these houses themselves are easily visible to the casual visitor. A selection of names to look out for. . .

RARC AN ILAN, CLIFF CASTLE, INNISCORRIG, ELSINORE and **LOTA** are all on Coliemore Road, as is one of the finest of all, **VICTORIA HOUSE.** This was built by one James Milo Burke, a significant operator in the development of the town. On the same road he also built **QUEENSTOWN CASTLE** and **SPRINGFIELD** and also, with a Dr MacDonnell, he built the present pier at Coliemore Harbour in 1847. This Dr MacDonnell, who was Provost of TCD, lived in the end house of what is now the much admired **SORRENTO TERRACE. MONTE ALVERNO** was built in its present form by Alexander Conan (who, incidentally, was the grandfather of this writer). Conan was also responsible for the creation of the adjoining **Sorrento Park.** In another part of Dalkey there is **HARVIESTON** on Cunningham Road, onetime home of Mr Eason, founder of the newsagent chain of that name.

WHAT'S IN A NAME ?

Placenames tell their own history throughout Ireland. An urban area such as Dalkey is no exception. Many names derive from families who at one time or another were important in the location. **ULVERTON ROAD** takes its name from the family Wolverston, English people who came to Ireland in the time of Edward VI. A house **Wolverton** on Barnhill Road is also associated with this family. This house is on the site of a place called in Gaelic times *Raheen*, meaning 'Little Rath'. A rath was a fortified farmstead.

BARNHILL ROAD may take its name from the Barnewall family, though there was also a large barn-like structure in this vicinity, possibly a Tithe Barn. **LESLIE AVENUE** takes its name from the Leslie family who built the house *Carraig na Greine*, a name which can be translated as 'Rock of The Sun'. Remembering that it is close to the site of the vanished stone circle this name may be traditional to the locality, though it may merely reflect the fashion of the time for Irish-language names for houses. **COLIEMORE ROAD** translates as 'Big Harbour Road'. **CORRIG ROAD** means rocky road or 'road through rocks', thus called because it is part of an alternative ancient coastal route from Monkstown Castle to Dalkey Harbour, the name occuring elsewhere along the route in DunLaoghaire. And the road names **ARDEEVIN, ARDBRUGH and KNOCKNACREE** all have meanings connected to hills and heights. **CARYSFORT ROAD** is called after the family of that title who owned property in Dalkey. **CUNNINGHAM ROAD** simply comes from the name of the builder, John Cunningham, who also gave his name to the house **John Ville**. **SORRENTO, NERANO** and **VICO** roads reflect the. interest in things Italian during their construction, also the feeling that somehow Dalkey was reminiscent of parts of Italy. Many individual houses in these roads also have Italian names. Names now forgotten include *Carrigetannail (sic)*, shown on early maps as being on the right hand side of the road coming to Dalkey from Dublin. This 'Rock of The Beacon' is probably the mound opposite Bullock Castle in the school grounds. Another name, *Pollnabroniagh*, appears on 19th century maps as an inlet near the Vico Bathing Place. Translated as 'Hole of The Giving', this name most likely derives from ancient sacrificial practices.

CARVED IN STONE...

Rathdown Slab: Taking its name from the nearby district of Rathdown, this slab is one of several peculiar to the area. The type of decoration is an apparant amalgam of pre-christian and early christian forms. The cupmarks and concentric circles are typical of pre-christian carving though the stone here is a *leac* or slab, rather than a boulder. A Welsh influence has been suggested. The Rathdown Slab is in the old cemetery in Castle Street.

Dalkey Island Petroglyph: A 'Greek', 'Eastern' or 'Scythian' cross is carved on a rock about eleven metres west of the church on Dalkey Island. (Another similar about 7 metres north).

The cross is a cross-within-circle of a type also found on islands off the west coast of Ireland. St Bega or Begnet *(see page 9)* is reputed to have had a cross inscribed bracelet and this carving may represent either that or have been the general symbol of some island dwelling mystical female sect.

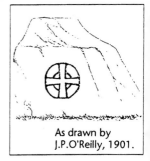

As drawn by
J.P.O'Reilly, 1901.

Dalkey Avenue Cross: On the railway bridge on Dalkey Avenue is a small stone cross, carved on to one of the stones let in to the wall on the left hand side ascending the hill. While the cross is perhaps only 150 years old, its story is interesting.

The original route from surrounding areas to the old cemetery was along the south side of the town, and this site would have been on the route and was most likely the crossing point of the Dalkey Stream. Up to quite recent times it was the custom for Dalkey funerals to divert and pause at this spot before proceeding to the place of burial. The custom long predates the railway and originally, it is said, the spot was marked by a wooden cross. Here people said 'stations', a type of praying while walking in circles. Throughout Ireland there are many similar locations where, for reasons lost in antiquity, funerals pause.

At some of these places people leave their own little wooden crosses and piles of these can be seen by the roadside.

Green Road Eagle: This stone bird was carved, apparently just for the hell of it, by two stonemasons named Cooper in the latter part of the 19th century. **The Green Road** itself is a pedestrian pathway parallel to but above the Vico Road. Accessible by steps ('The Cat's Ladder') from there, or by car from Torca Road or Burma Road carpark, it skirts the eastern side of Dalkey Hill and affords magnificent views. These views are the reasons for the road's existence, it being laid out to facilitate the carriage of a visiting English monarch.

Dalkey Island and Sorrento, an 1869 lithograph of the view from the Green Road.

The Nerano Sailor: Carved in concrete rather than stone, this larger than life figure is some 150 years old and may have been originally erected by the retired mariner who lived in the house in earlier years. Nerano is a private house on the road of the same name but the sailor can easily be spotted from the roads around.

Hogan's Nativity: John Hogan (died 1858) was one of Ireland's finest sculptors, noted particularly for his Dublin statues, of Daniel O'Connell in the City Hall, and that of The Dead Christ in Clarendon Street Church. The Nativity carving on the altar in the chapel of Loreto Abbey in Dalkey is his work. Loreto Abbey complex of buildings, now a large girls' school, is approached *via* Harbour Road.

WELLS

There are many ancient wells around Dalkey, mostly now forgotten since they fell into disuse with the advent of piped water. Two of these at least were 'holy wells', both dedicated to St Begnet. Holy Wells auch as these are found throughout Ireland, and many people still have great devotion to them and respect for their healing powers. Practically all Holy Wells are pre-Christian in origin and their existence harks back to ancient beliefs.

St Begnet's Well, Dalkey Island:
Up to the early part of the 19th century this was known as Scurvey Well, and was regarded as a cure for that and other ailments. Scurvey was of course common amongst seafarers and thus appropriate for a well in a major port. In later years the well has been regarded as a cure for the eyes, though this repute is common to many Dublin wells and may merely be a result of folklore confusion.

St Begnet's Well, Dalkey Town: This well was perhaps the original St Begnet's Well, now unfortunately buried beneath concrete at the end of Tramway Lane. This (unmarked) walkway runs off Castle Street beside the Health Centre and is so-called because, in the days of Tram, the Tramway Office was in the presentday pharmacy on the corner. There was also a urinal for tram workers situed at the end of the lane. At the Holy Well!

Ordinary wells with no religious significance include

Tubbermore Road Well, in the town, on a road which takes its name from the Irish, translated as 'Big Well Road'. The site of the well is at the old pump in the brick archway.

Dillons Park Well: On Coliemore Road in the park of that name.

Goat Castle Well: In Castle Street, beneath the floor of La Romana restaurant.

The Well of The Gallion: On the top of Dalkey Hill, now quarried away. *(illus.opposite, from a 1776 drawing by Gabriel Beranger).*

*Wells also existed on the north side of the **Shell Garage**, on the East side of the **Catholic Church**,(more or less under the trees), and opposite the entrance to **Hillside Estate** at the bottom of The Flags on Dalkey Avenue.*

TREASURE!

On the following pages there is the outline of a Dalkey treasure hunt. Even less well known is the story of an actual discovery of treasure hidden in Dalkey. In 1838 people were demolishing the gatepillars to a property known as Castle House, beside the present-day Queen's Pub. In a hollow section of the stonework they found hidden a hoard of coins. These, of silver, turned out to be tenth century Anglo-Saxon, from the reign of Eadgar. There were around sixty five in number, and the majority ended up in the British Museum where they remain as an intact collection. Certain numismatic opinion has it that many of the coins were of a special type, struck particularly for trade between Chester and Norse settlements.

How exactly they ended up in the British Museum is obscure but not unknown. Antiquarians, like all specialists, protect their own and have not delved too deeply into the involvement of George Petrie, a major 19th century antiquarian. The harsh facts appear to be that the workmen who found the coins gave them, probably for a few pints of beer, to a local gentleman who in turn gave them to Petrie as a present. Petrie, broke at the time, said nothing publicly but, after a delicate interval, sold them through an intermediary to the museum.

Above, Dalkey Coin in British Museum;
Below, Cloch Tobair Gailline, (see previous page).

ABOUT A DALKEY WITCH. . .

Etty Scott was the daughter of one of the skilled workers from Scotland who came to Dalkey to work in the quarries during the construction of DunLaoghaire Harbour. Although she was reputed never to smile, she was regarded as beautiful. With long black hair, she had a 'well-proportioned figure', and she carried a knife or dagger in 'an ample bosom'.

Etty was prey to visions and prophetic dreams and, when in a trance-like condition, she would recite these to the simple labourers who lived in cabins around the area. On occasion, taking the knife from her bodice, she would decapitate a chicken and sprinkle blood about the place. There is no record as to what precisely she believed in or to what purposes she applied her magic, though we can be sure she didn't belong to the mainstream of Victorian Christianity!

One day she announced that she had a vision of buried treasure. This, she explained, was a forgotten horde left behind by the Vikings. The logic of her vision was that, Dalkey being a port, it was a place where Vikings and invaders would gather their pillage together before transporting it back to their homelands.

The labourers weren't so simple that they didn't prefer the prospect of treasure to that of quarrying stone! Crowds of them abandoned work and, following Etty's instructions, spent considerable energies, and a significant amount of their employers' dynamite, in quarrying along the shoreline in the search.

Beautiful large breasted witches who decapitate chickens with arcane incantations were no more popular with the authorities in those times than they might be now. When their behaviour results in social unrest they become even less popular. And so it was that Etty began to come in for adverse official comment.

At that time, just as now in fact, students and other middleclass riff raff from Dublin were in the habit of drinking in Dalkey's many taverns. The town had a Yukon Gold Rush atmosphere created by the huge influx of seriously drinking quarry workers, plus the associated crowds of chancers and harlots and other colourful folks who, incidentally, are the ancestors of the modern Dalkey citizenry.

Etty's own personal gold rush came to an end when a group of these students, encouraged no doubt by Government spies, created a ludicrous diversion by setting fires to cats and releasing them amongst her followers at night. This caused particular consternation because the labourers had been keyed up, by Etty's Prophecy, about the imminent arrival of a 'Great Spirit Entity'. The mad burning cats hurtling about the place confused the issues and the gold rush petered away.

Etty later married a medical student and the young couple went to England to escape, it was said, the outrage of his parents. She returned to Dalkey many years later, a widow with apparently substantial means. With her was one of her grown-up children, a pregnant young woman. The return to Ireland, it was said, was to escape scandal about the unmarried daughter's condition. This child in turn, a girl, married into a Dalkey family which, to this day, has somewhat of a reputation for association with the 'Black Arts'.

Etty Scott's onetime cottage occupied the site of a house called Geraldine, on Sorrento Road, in recent years renamed 'The L.O.G.'

The horde of treasure (still undiscovered to this day) is, according to Etty's visions, buried along the shoreline where the houses Inniscorrig and Elsinore on Coliemore Road are now built. (Treasure hunters should seek permission before digging here).

. . .AND A DALKEY GHOST. . .

Along the lower road beside Bullock Harbour *(right opposite utility pole number 22)* there is the outline of an archway in the stone wall, the opening within now itself blocked with masonry. This was part of a route through to the Bullock Wells and, on occasion, a female ghost can be seen passing back and forth between the stones. In the nearby vicinity the lower end of Castlepark Road is also said to be haunted.

FAMOUS RESIDENTS OF DALKEY...

While practically everybody in Ireland is famous for at least five minutes in their lifetime, Dalkey is home to many who have overstayed their welcome in the limelight. Prominent media, arts and entertainment people are thick on the streets. While it is a tradition in the town to ignore famous residents until they're dead, a tradition which this guide will uphold. residents of previous eras can be safely discussed.

JOHN DOWLAND *(died 1626)* was born in Dalkey. The greatest lute player of his time, he travelled extensively in Europe and was at one time Court Lutanist to the King of Denmark. The 17th Century equivalent of a megastar, his songs and melodies were widely known. Dowland was a friend of Shakespeare and it has been suggested that the playwright based his description of the cliff's of Hamlet's Elsinore on Dowland's stories of Dalkey. Whatever about that, it is a fact that Shakespeare is a well-known surname in Dalkey to this day.
There is a mosaic memorial to Dowland in Sorrento Park.

EDWARD CARSON *(died 1935)* was a Dubliner and lived in Dalkey before going on to become a noted lawyer and, more memorably, the leader of the Irish Unionists and founder of the Ulster Volunteers.
Carson lived in Monte Alverno, Sorrento Road, but at a time when that house was considerably less grandiose and in fact two separate dwellings.

JAMES JOYCE (died 1941**)** was a schoolteacher for a period in a private school in Dalkey.
This school was situated in the house called Summerfield, on Dalkey Avenue.

GEORGE BERNARD SHAW *(died 1950)* spent summers in Dalkey. Shaw's parents had a friend, Mr Lee, who lived with them in a genteel polyandric arrangement. Lee taught the mother music and eventually decamped with her to London, young George following a few years later. In Dalkey Lee owned a cottage and Shaw spent many childhood summers there. In later life he wrote of the place with fond memories.
'Shaw's Cottage '(private) is on Torca Road.

... AND THREE GOOD PLACES TO EAT

The Queen's Restaurant.
The Vico
(see below),
and P.D.'s Woodhouse
(see next page and back cover).

The Queens

Established in 1745, "The Queen's" is one of Ireland's oldest hostelries. At the heart of Dalkey, our award winning pub carries on the finest tradition of providing the very best in cuisine, convivial enjoyment and service in a unique atmosphere.

Our two restaurants present different styles of cooking - the downstairs QUEEN'S RESTAURANT offers popular modern Mediterranean selections, while THE VICO upstairs gives you the choice of an international style cuisine with a modern flair.

TEL: 01 2854569

P. D.'s Woodhouse

THE ORIGINAL OAKWOOD BARBEQUE BISTRO

This book is part of the

FACT PACK

series produced by
MORRIGAN BOOKS
Ireland's leading publishers of Local History
Potential authors or readers can contact us at
morrigan@online.ie

Conan Kennedy's books include
(non-fiction)
ANCIENT IRELAND - A USER'S GUIDE
PLACES OF MYTHOLOGY
LOOKING FOR DE SELBY
(and fiction)
HERE BE GHOSTS
OGULLA WELL